The Little
Book of

COCKNEY RHYMING SLANG

The Little
Book of

COCKNEY
RHYMING
SLANG

Betty Kirkpatrick

Michael O'Mara Humour

First published in Great Britain in 2001 by
Michael O'Mara Books Limited
9 Lion Yard
Tremadoc Road
London SW4 7NQ

A CIP catalogue record for this book is available from
the British Library

ISBN 1-84317-027-2

3 5 7 9 10 8 6 4

Designed and typeset by Design 23

Printed and bound in Great Britain
by William Clowes, Beccles, Suffolk

INTRODUCTION

Cockney rhyming slang is a variety of idiomatic speech in which a particular word is replaced with a phrase of two or three words which rhymes with it. The slang originated in London and some of the rhymes are true rhymes only if they are sounded in line with Cockney pronunciation.

This form of slang is almost certainly not as old as we might assume, the likelihood being that it came into existence at the beginning of the twentieth century. It should be remembered, however, that ascribing precise dates to language can be very difficult, particularly language like rhyming slang, which was originally handed on by word of mouth.

The reason for the rise of Cockney rhyming slang is not all that clear either, but there is a distinct possibility that it came into being as a means of keeping the police ignorant of what was happening around them. Thus rhyming slang might well have been originally a kind of code used by criminal groups, such as vagabonds, thieves and the less honest street sellers, to pass on secret information to each other.

There is an element of humour and ingenuity about much rhyming slang and so it was gradually taken up by other people, originally members of the working classes, who had not necessarily anything to hide from the police. It even left the confines of London with people who emigrated from there, and made its way to Australia and America.

Sometimes the slang was, and is, used as a kind of euphemism for words relating to subjects that might cause embarrassment – bodily functions, for example. The rhymes often refer to people who are or were topical at the time the rhyming phrase was coined, and not infrequently the phrase outlasts their popularity. Thus rhyming slang easily becomes obscure.

Nevertheless, rhyming slang has not only survived the decades, but it is currently enjoying something of a revival; a revival seemingly helped by the Internet. This is particularly true among young people who may feel attracted to its inventiveness and its irreverence. Cockney rhyming slang tends to be at the opposite end of the spectrum from politically correct language.

This book gives a selection of examples of Cockney rhyming slang, both old and new. Its very size prevents it from being comprehensive, so my apologies if your own particular favourite is missing. Still, it's worth a butcher's hook.

RHYMING SLANG – ENGLISH
ABC

I was watching the custard and jelly the other night when the ginger pops came bursting in my cat and mouse and nicked my Chelsea bun.

A

Abergavenny a penny

Abraham Lincoln stinking

Adam and Eve believe

Alan Whickers knickers (Alan Whicker [b. 1925], British TV personality)

airs and graces 1 faces 2 braces 3 horse races

apples, apples and pears stairs

apple tart a fart

Aristotle a bottle

artful dodger lodger (a character in *Oliver Twist* [1839], a novel by Charles Dickens [1812-70])

Arthur Rank 1 bank (financial) 2 act of masturbation (vulgar slang **wank**) (J. Arthur, Lord Rank [1888-1972], British film magnate)

Auntie Ella umbrella

Auntie Nellie stomach (informal **belly**)

Ayrton Senna ten pounds sterling (informal **tenner**) (Brazilian racing driver, three times F1 world Champion [1960-94])

B

babbling brook crook, criminal
baby's pram jam
backseat driver lazy person (slang **skiver**)
bacon and eggs legs
bacon rind blind
Baden-Powell trowel (Robert, Lord Baden-Powell [1857-1941], soldier, founder of the Scout movement)
bag of flour shower (of rain)
bag of fruit a suit
bag of yeast priest
baker's dozen cousin
ball and bat hat
ball of chalk 1 a walk 2 a talk
ball of lead head
Band of Hope soap (a British temperance society formed in 1847)

bangers and mash **1** act of urinating (vulgar slang **slash**) **2** cash

Barnaby Rudge a judge (a character in the novel of the same name [1841] by Charles Dickens [1812-70])

barnet, Barnet Fair hair (a major horse fair held in Barnet, Greater London, from the sixteenth to the eighteenth centuries)

bar of soap cannabis (slang **dope**)

bat and wicket ticket

bath bun **1** son **2** the sun

battle cruiser pub (slang **boozer**)

bazaar bar (drinking establishment)

bees and honey money

beg your pardon a garden

bell-ringers fingers

bended knees cheese

Benny Hill **1** drill **2** till (cash) (British comedian [1925-92])

berk, Berkeley Hunt stupid, foolish or annoying person (vulgar slang **cunt**)

Bernie Flint penniless (slang **skint**)

Betty Grable table (US film star [1916-73])

Bexleyheath teeth (town in Greater London)

Big Ben 1 ten 2 ten pounds sterling

big bloke cocaine (slang **coke**)

big dippers slippers

Billy Bunter ordinary person, customer, someone who bets (slang **punter**) (a large and foolish schoolboy, the principal character in the 'Greyfriars' novels of Frank Richards [1876-1961])

billy goat a coat

Billy Liar tyre (the title of a novel [1959] by Keith Waterhouse [b. 1929], later filmed)

bird, birdlime prison sentence (slang **time**)

biscuits and cheese knees

Black & Decker penis (vulgar slang **pecker**) (the trade name of a manufacturer of power tools)

blindman's buff snuff (tobacco)

blue moon a spoon

board and plank an American (slang Yank)

boat and oar prostitute (**whore**)

bob and dick 1 sick 2 penis (vulgar slang **dick, prick, wick**)

Bob Hope cannabis (slang **dope**) (US comedian and film star [b. 1903])

booed and hissed drunk (vulgar slang **pissed**)

boots and socks venereal disease (informal **pox**)

bo peep 1 sleep 2 a peep (glimpse, look) (from the nursery rhyme 'Little Bo Peep')

boracic, boracic lint penniless (slang **skint**)

born and bred bed

borrow and beg egg

bottle nerve, courage (from **bottle and glass**, vulgar slang **arse**, since someone who is terrified is thought likely to foul himself; hence **to lose one's bottle**

means to give way to nerves or fear)

bottle and stopper police officer (slang **copper**)

bottle of beer ear

bottle of porter daughter

bottle of sauce a horse

bottle of scent effeminate, homosexual (slang **bent**)

bottle of water daughter

bottle of wine a fine (penalty)

bow and arrow 1 sparrow 2 barrow 3 charabanc (informal **chara**)

bow and quiver liver

Brahms and Liszt drunk (vulgar slang **pissed**) (the composers [German and Hungarian, respectively] Johannes Brahms [1833-97] and Franz Liszt [1811-86])

brandy snap a slap

brass band hand

brass tacks facts

brave and bold cold

bread and cheese a sneeze

bread and honey money
bread and lard hard
bread knife wife
Brenda Frickers knickers (Brenda Fricker [b. 1944], Irish actress)
Brian Clough rough (British football manager [b. 1935])
Brian O'Flynn gin
bricks and mortar daughter
Brighton Pier 1 queer 2 to disappear, leave or run away
Brighton rock the dock (in a courtroom)
Bristol, Bristol city female breast (vulgar slang **titty**)
British Rail e-mail
Britney Spears beers (US pop singer [b. 1981])
broken heart a fart
broken quiver liver
brother and sister a blister
Brown Bess yes (British military musket used during the Napoleonic Wars)

brown bread dead

Brown Joe no

Brussels sprout Boy Scout

bubble and squeak 1 a Greek 2 week
3 act of urinating (vulgar slang **leak**)

bubble bath a laugh

bubble gum buttocks (informal **bum**)

Bugs Bunny money (a Warner Brothers
cartoon-film character, created in 1940)

bull and cow row (quarrel, argument)

Bunsen burner profit-making scheme
(informal **earner**)

burglar alarm arm

Burlington Bertie thirty ('Burlington
Bertie from Bow', a popular song [1915]
by W. F. Hargreaves [1846-1919])

burnt cinder window

Burton-on-Trent rent

bushel and peck neck

Buster Keaton meeting (US silent-film
comedian [1895-1966])

butcher's, butcher's hook a look, glance

buttered bread dead
buttered bun one (number)
buttons and bows toes

C

cab rank bank (financial)
Cain and Abel table
Calcutta butter
Calvin Klein 1 fine (penalty) 2 wine
  3 nine (US fashion designer [b. 1942])
canal boat the tote (state betting system)
can of Coke a joke
can of oil a boil (spot)
Captain Bligh a pie (William Bligh [*c.*
  1753-1817], captain of HMS *Bounty*, the
  crew of which mutinied in 1789)
Captain Cook 1 a look 2 a book (James
  Cook [1728-79], British navigator and
  explorer)
captain's log toilet (slang **bog**)
cardboard box venereal disease

(informal **pox**)

car park police informer (slang **nark**)

carving knife wife

cash and carried married

cat and mouse a house

Cecil Gee knee (chain of menswear shops)

chain and locket a pocket

Charing Cross horse

chalfonts haemorrhoids (informal **piles**) (Chalfont St Giles, village in Buckinghamshire)

Charles Dance a chance (British film, TV and stage actor [b. 1946])

Charles James 1 theatre box 2 a fox (Charles James Fox [1749-1806], British Whig politician, statesman and orator)

Charley Frisky whisky

Charley Howard coward

Charley Mason 1 basin 2 basinful (i.e. a great deal; too much of)

Charley Randy brandy

Charley Skinner dinner

Charlie Drake 1 a break, free time 2 vehicle brake (British comedian [b. 1925])

Charlie Prescott waistcoat

Charlie Pride a ride (on horseback, in a car etc.)

Charlie Ronce a pimp (slang **ponce**)

Charlie Smirke stupid or foolish person (vulgar rhyming slang **berk** [q.v.])

charming wife a knife

Chatham and Dover to stop doing something (slang **give over**) (towns in Kent)

cheese and crackers testicles (vulgar slang **knackers**)

cheese and rice Jesus Christ (as an oath)

cheese grater waiter

Cheesy Quaver a favour (trade name of a kind of savoury snack)

Chelsea bun 1 son 2 the sun

Cheltenham gold cold (Cheltenham Gold Cup, a National Hunt race meeting)

cherrypicker one pound sterling (slang

nicker)

cherry red head

Chevy Chase face (sixteenth-century English ballad about a Border battle between Scots and English)

chicken and rice nice

chicken's neck cheque

china, china plate friend (informal **mate**)

chips and peas knees

chopping sticks six

chorus and verse buttocks, anus (vulgar slang **arse**)

Christmas crackered exhausted (slang **knackered**)

Christmas Eve believe

Christopher Lee act of urinating (informal **pee**) (British film actor [b. 1922])

Cilla Black the back (British singer and TV personality [b. 1943])

Claire Rayner trainer (shoe) (British agony aunt and novelist [b. 1931]

Clark Kent corrupt (slang **bent**) (the pseudonym of the comic-strip character Superman in his ordinary life)

clever Mike bicycle (**bike**)

clickety-click sixty-six

clothes pegs legs

club and stick detective (US slang **dick**)

coat and badge to cadge

cobblers, cobbler's awls 1 testicles (vulgar slang **balls**) 2 nonsense, rubbish

cob o'coal dole (unemployment benefit)

cock and hen, cockle and hen 1 ten 2 ten pounds

cock linnet a minute (time)

cod's roe money (slang **dough**)

cold potato waiter

collar and tie a lie (untruth)

Colonel Gaddafi café (Moamar Muhammad al-Gaddafi [b. 1942], Libyan leader [1969-])

comb and brush alcoholic drink, an alcoholic (slang **lush**)

Conan Doyle a boil (spot) (Sir Arthur
  Conan Doyle [1859-1930], novelist and
  creator of Sherlock Holmes)
conger eel tell on, inform (on someone
  to) a person in authority (slang **squeal**)
constant screamer concertina
corned beef 1 thief **2** chief prison officer
corns and bunions onions
cough and choke to smoke (cigarettes
  etc.)
cough and sneeze cheese
cough and stutter butter
country cousin dozen
cow and calf 1 a laugh **2** half
cow's lick prison (slang **nick**)
cream cookie bookmaker (slang **bookie**)
cream crackered exhausted (slang
  knackered)
cream puff bad temper (**huff**)
Crimea beer (from the Crimean War
  [1853-6], in which Britain, France,
  Turkey and Sardinia fought Russia)

crowded space suitcase
crown jewels tools
crust of bread head
currant bread dead
currant bun 1 son 2 the sun
custard and jelly television (informal **telly**)

DEF

I was chatting to me soap and lather on the dog and bone when I suddenly let out an enormous bread and cheese.

D

daft and barmy army

daily bread head (of the family)

daisy beat to cheat, swindle

daisy roots boots

Damon Hill pill (British racing driver [b. 1960])

dancing fleas keys

Danny La Rue clue, idea (the stage name of British entertainer and female impersonator Daniel Patrick Carroll [b. 1927])

Darby and Joan 1 telephone (**phone**) 2 alone (idealized elderly couple, from an eighteenth-century English ballad)

Darby Kelly stomach (informal **belly**)

Darren Gough a cough (English cricketer [b. 1970])

David Gower shower (of rain) (English cricketer [b. 1957])

Davy Crockett a pocket (US lawyer, politician, frontiersman and soldier [1786-1836])

dead horse tomato sauce

deep-sea diver five pounds sterling (informal **fiver**)

Desmond a lower-second (informal 'Two-two') university degree (Desmond Tutu [b. 1931], South African clergyman and political activist)

deuce and ace face

dicky-bird word

didn't ought port (wine)

didn't oughter water

dig a grave to shave

dirty daughter water

do as you like a bicycle (**bike**)

doctor and nurse purse

Doctor Crippen dripping (fat) (Dr Hawley Harvey Crippen [1862-1910], US-born British murderer)

dog and bone telephone (**phone**)

dog's, dog's meat feet

Dolly Cotton rotten

dolly mixtures cinema (the **pictures**) (small, coloured sweets sold as a mixture)

Dolly Varden a garden (a character in the novel *Barnaby Rudge* [1841] by Charles Dickens [1812-70])

Donald Trump bowel movement (vulgar slang **dump**) (US property developer [b. 1946])

don't make a fuss bus

door-to-door four

dot and carry marry

dot and dash cash

Douglas Hurd 1 lump of excrement (vulgar slang **turd**) 2 third-class university degree (**Third**) (Douglas, Lord Hurd [b. 1930], British Conservative politician)

down the drain brain

D'Oyly Carte a fart (Richard D'Oyly Carte [1844-1901], impresario, founder [1875] of an opera company noted for its performances of the works of Gilbert and Sullivan)

dripping toast publican (informal/facetious **mine host**)

drum and bass home (**place**)

drum and fife 1 a knife 2 wife

Dublin trick a brick

Duchess of Fife wife

Duke of Kent 1 rent 2 homosexual (slang **bent**)

Duke of York 1 fork 2 talk 3 chalk (for billiards and snooker cues) 4 walk 5 pork

Dunlop tyre liar

dustbin lid child (informal **kid**)

Dutch pegs legs

Dutch, Dutch plate friend (informal **mate**)

E

early bird word

Eartha Kitt bowel movement (vulgar slang **shit**) (US singer and actress [b. 1928])

earwig understand (slang **twig**)

east and south mouth

east and west vest

Easter bunny money

Easter egg leg

eau de cologne telephone (**phone**)

egg yoke a joke

Eiffel Tower shower (of rain)

Elephant and Castle anus (vulgar slang **arsehole**) (district in South London; the name is said to derive from a visit of the Infanta of Castile)

elephant's trunk drunk

Epsom races 1 braces 2 faces

Errol Flynn chin (Australian-born film star [1909-59])

F

false alarm arm

Farmer Giles haemorrhoids (informal
  piles)

fiddle and flute a suit

fife and drum buttocks (informal **bum**)

fine and dandy brandy

finger and thumb 1 rum 2 keep quiet
  (**mum**) 3 friend (informal **chum**)
  4 a drum

fisherman's daughter water

flea and louse 1 house 2 brothel
  (informal **house [of ill repute]**)

fleas and ants trousers, pants

flounder and dab taxi (**cab**)

flowery dell prison cell

fly-by-nights tights

flying trapeze cheese

fly-tipper child (informal **nipper**)

fore and aft daft

fork and knife 1 wife 2 life

Fortnum and Mason 1 basin 2 pudding

basin (famous store in Central London, noted for its food department)

forty-four 1 prostitute (**whore**) 2 door-to-door salesman

France and Spain rain

Frank Bough stale, rotting (informal **off**) (British sports commentator [b. 1933])

fridge freezer person, man (slang **geezer**)

frisk and frolic soap (originally **carbolic** soap)

frock and frill a chill

frog and toad road

frog in the throat boat

fun and frolics testicles (vulgar slang **bollocks**)

GHI

A forty-four came to my Rory O'Moore to try and sell me some Captain Cooks. When I told him no go, he let out a horse and cart and scarpered!

G

garden gate **1** friend (informal **mate**)
   2 magistrate **3** eight
garden gnome a comb
garden plant aunt
Gary Glitter **1** pint of bitter (beer) **2** anus
   (vulgar slang **shitter**) (stage name of
   British pop singer Paul Gadd [b. 1940])
gay and frisky whisky
gay and hearty a party
Gay Gordon traffic warden
general election erection
Geoff Hurst **1** first-class university degree
   (**First**) **2** a thirst **3** burst (English
   footballer [b. 1941])
Gert and Daisy lazy (characters in a radio
   show created by British comediennes
   Elsie and Doris Waters in the 1930s)
giggle and titter pint of bitter (beer)
ginger ale gaol
ginger beer **1** queer (strange)
   2 homosexual (informal **queer**)

34

ginger pop police officer (slang **cop**)

giraffe laugh

give and get a bet

glass of beer ear

Glenn Hoddle something simple (informal **doddle**) (British football manager and former player [b. 1957])

glory be tea

God forbid 1 child (informal **kid**) 2 hat (informal **lid**)

God in heaven seven

gold watch Scotch (whisky)

gone to bed dead

goose and duck sexual intercourse (vulgar slang **fuck**)

goose's neck cheque

grease and grime time

greengages wages

Gregory Peck 1 neck 2 cheque (US film star [b. 1916])

grey mare a fare (bus, train, etc.)

grumble and mutter a bet (informal

flutter)

guinea pig wig

Gypsy Rose Lee tea (stage name of the US actress, striptease artiste and author Rose Louise Hovick [1914-70])

gypsy's kiss act of urinating (vulgar slang **piss**)

H

haddock and bloater car (informal **motor**)

hair gel bell

hairy knees please

hale and hearty party

half-inch steal (informal **pinch**)

ham and bone 1 home 2 telephone (informal **phone**)

ham and cheesy easy

hammer and discus whiskers (beard etc.)

Hampstead Heath teeth (area of park

and woodland in North London)

hampton, Hampton Wick penis (vulgar slang **prick**) (village in Greater London)

ham shank an American (slang **Yank**)

hand and fist drunk (vulgar slang **pissed**)

Hank Marvin starving (British pop guitarist [b. 1941])

happy hour 1 flower 2 shower (of rain)

harbour light all right

hard and flat a hat

hare and hound round (of drinks)

Harold Macmillan villain (1st Earl of Stockton [1894-1986], British Conservative politician; Prime Minister [1957-63])

Harry Tate 1 late 2 plate 3 eight (British stage comedian [1872-1940])

Harvey Nichols pickles (well-known Central London department store)

hat and scarf a bath

haystack the back

heart of oak penniless (slang **broke**)

heaven and hell smell
heavens above love
Henrietta a letter
here and there chair
herring and kipper striptease artiste (stripper)
hide and seek cheek (impertinence)
Highland fling 1 string 2 a ring 3 sing
high seas knees
high-stepper pepper
hit and miss 1 a kiss 2 urine (vulgar slang piss)
hit and run the sun
Holy Ghost 1 the post (mail) 2 the starting or winning post on a racecourse 3 toast
Hong Kong 1 wrong 2 a smell (slang **pong**)
horn of plenty twenty
horse and cart 1 heart 2 a fart
hot and cold gold
hot dinner a winner
hot toddy the body

House of Fraser razor (chain of department stores)

house to let a bet

Howard's Way gay, homosexual (TV serial of the 1980s)

hugs and kisses wife (informal **missus**)

hurricane lamp a tramp

husband and wife a knife

Hush Puppy a yuppie (the trade name of a brand of shoes)

Hyde Park police informer (slang **nark**) (large park in Central London)

I

ice-cream freezer man, person (slang **geezer**)

ideal home a comb

inky blue influenza (**flu**)

insects and ants trousers (**pants**)

inside right mean (informal **tight**)

in the mood food

in the nude food
Irish jig wig
Irish stew true
iron girder murder
Iron Mike bicycle (**bike**)
iron tank bank (financial)
Isle of Wight 1 right, all right 2 light
  3 mean (informal **tight**)
itch and scratch a match (**light**)
ivory pearl girl

JKL

My best finger and thumb played the Joanna
at my bottle of water's wedding last year.
We kicked and pranced through the night.

J

Jack and Jill 1 hill 2 pill 3 till (cash)

Jackanory story (children's TV series in which stories were read aloud)

Jack Jones, on one's alone, on one's own

jack of spades sunglasses (slang **shades**)

Jack's alive five

Jackson Pollocks testicles (vulgar slang **bollocks**) (US artist [1912-56])

jack tar bar (drinking establishment)

jack the lad bad

Jack the Ripper 1 kipper 2 slipper (name given to a British serial murderer, never identified, who killed and mutilated at least seven prostitutes in London's East End [August-November 1888])

Jagger's lips chips (Mick Jagger [b. 1943], British rock star)

jam jar car

jam roll 1 parole 2 dole (unemployment benefit)

jar of jam 1 pram 2 tram

Jasper Carrott a parrot (British comedian [b. 1945])

jellied eels transport, especially a car (informal **wheels**)

Jennie Lee 1 tea 2 key 3 flea (Baroness Lee of Asheridge [1904-88], Scottish Labour politician, wife of Aneurin Bevan [1897-1960])

Jenny Lind wind (flatulence) (Swedish soprano [1820-87])

Jeremiah a fire

Jimmy Hill a pill (British football commentator [b. 1928])

Jimmy Nail 1 stale 2 a sale 3 mail (British actor and singer [b. 1954])

Jimmy Riddle act of urinating (informal **piddle**)

Jimmy Skinner dinner

Jimmy Young 1 tongue 2 bribe (slang **bung**) (British singer and radio presenter [b. 1923])

Joanna piano

jockey's whip 1 sleep (slang **kip**) 2 chip (potato)

Jodrell Bank act of masturbation (vulgar slang **wank**)

Joe Baxi taxi

Joe Blake 1 steak 2 snake

Joe Brown town (British pop singer and actor [b. 1941])

Joe McBride sexual intercourse (slang **ride**)

Joe Roke a cigarette break (informal **smoke**)

Joe Soap a fool (informal **dope**)

John Cleese cheese (British actor and comedian [b. 1939])

John Major a wager (British Conservative politician [b. 1943]; Prime Minister [1990-7])

Johnnie Walker talker, informer (popular brand of whisky)

John Wayne train (stage name of Marion

Michael Morrison, US film star [1907-79])

Jolly Roger lodger

joy of my life wife

Judi Dench stench (Dame Judi Dench, British actress and stage director [b. 1934])

jug and pail gaol

Julian Clary a male homosexual (slang **fairy**) (British entertainer [b. 1959])

K

Kate Carney army (British music-hall star [1869-1950])

Ken Dodd roll of banknotes (informal **wad**) (British comedian and singer [b. 1931])

kick and prance a dance

King Canutes boots (Canute [Cnut] [*c.* 955-1035], Danish king of England [1016-35], Denmark [1018-35] and Norway [1028-35], who supposedly tried to hold back the tide)

King Death bad breath
kingdom come 1 rum 2 buttocks
(informal **bum**)
King Lear 1 ear 2 homosexual (informal
queer) (from the play [*c.* 1605] by
William Shakespeare [1564-1616])
kings and queens baked beans
kipper and plaice face
kiss and cuddle a muddle
kiss of life wife
kitchen sink a drink (alcoholic)
knobbly knee key
knock at the door four
knocker and knob job
kung-fu fighter cigarette lighter

L

la-di-dah 1 cigar 2 car
Lady Godiva 1 five 2 five pounds
(informal **fiver**) ([?1040-80] wife of
Leofric, Earl of Mercia; said to have

ridden naked through Coventry to
persuade her husband to lift taxes
imposed on the townspeople)

Lambeth Walk chalk (for billiards and
snooker cues) (dance – and song –
popularized by the musical *Me and My
Gal* [1932]; from the name of a street in
Lambeth, South London)

lame duck sexual intercourse (vulgar
slang **fuck**)

lath and plaster employer (**master**)

laugh and joke a cigarette break (informal
smoke)

laugh and titter a pint of bitter (beer)

lean and fat a hat

Lee Marvin very hungry (**starving**)
(US film star [1924-87])

left and right a fight

leg of beef thief

lemon curd 1 lump of excrement (vulgar
slang **turd**) 2 girl, young woman (slang
bird)

Len Hutton button (Sir Leonard Hutton, English cricketer [1916-90])

Leslie Ash, go for a urinate (vulgar slang **go for a slash**) (British actress [b. 1960])

Lester Piggott bigot (British flat-racing jockey [b. 1935])

life and death breath

Lillian Gish 1 dish 2 fish 3 urine (vulgar slang **pish**) (stage name of Lillian de Guiche, US film and stage actress [1899-1993])

Lionel Bart a fart (British composer and playwright [1930-99])

Lionel Blair 1 chair 2 mare (British entertainer [b. 1931])

Lionel Blairs flared trousers (informal **flares**) (see preceding entry)

lion's roar a snore

little and large margarine (informal **marge**)

Little Peter meter (for gas, electricity etc.)

loaf, loaf of bread head

London fog dog

loop the loop soup
lord and mastered drunk (slang **plastered)**
lord mayor to swear (curse)
Lorna Doone spoon (the heroine of a novel
  [1869] of the same name by R. D.
  Blackmore [1825-1900])
love and kisses wife (informal **missus**)
lucky charm arm
lump and bump fool (informal **chump)**
lump of ice advice

MNO

Last week my trouble and strife was
making some needle and thread, but
accidentally added in some frisk and
frolic. Boy did we Wallace and Gromit
when we ate our sandwiches that night!

M

macaroni twenty-five pounds sterling (slang **pony**)

Mae West female breast (US film star [1892-1980])

Mahatma Gandhi 1 brandy 2 shandy 3 randy (Mohandas Karamchand Gandhi, Indian social reformer and spiritual and political leader [1869-1948])

man alive five

man and wife a knife

marbles and conkers mad, crazy (slang **bonkers**)

Mars and Venus penis

Mars Bar a scar

Maud and Ruth truth

Max Walls testicles (vulgar slang **balls**) (Max Wall, British comedian [1908-90])

Melvyn Bragg sexual intercourse (vulgar slang **shag**) (Melvyn, Lord Bragg, British novelist and TV presenter [b. 1939])

merchant banker masturbator (vulgar

slang **wanker**), used as a general term of abuse

merry old soul 1 coal 2 a hole

Michael Caine 1 pain 2 stain (Sir Michael Caine, British film actor [b. 1933])

Michael Winner dinner (British film director and restaurant critic [b. 1935])

Mike Malone telephone (**phone**)

Milky Way homosexual (informal **gay**)

miller's daughter water

minces, mince pies eyes

moan and wail gaol

Moby Dick sick (the white whale in the novel [1851] of the same name by US writer Herman Melville [1819-91])

Molly McGuire a fire

monkey's cousin twelve (a **dozen**)

more or less a dress

Mother Hubbard cupboard

Mother Kelly 1 jelly 2 television (informal **telly**)

Mutt and Jeff deaf (US cartoon

characters created by H. C. 'Bud' Fischer in the 1930s)

mutter and stutter butter

Mystic Meg leg (British popular astrologer formerly involved in the broadcasting of the National Lottery results)

N

Nancy Lee 1 tea 2 flea

nanny goat 1 a coat 2 boat 3 throat 4 the tote (state betting system)

Nat King Cole the dole (unemployment benefit) (US popular singer [1919-65])

needle and pin 1 gin 2 thin

needle and thread bread

needles and pins twins

Nelson Eddies cash (slang **the readies**) (Nelson Eddy, US popular singer [1901-67])

nervous wreck cheque

never fear pint of beer

Niagara Falls testicles (vulgar slang **balls**)

night and day a play (drama)

Noah's ark **1** lark (prank) **2** lark (bird) **3** park **4** informer (slang **nark**) **5** shark

Nobby Stiles haemorrhoids (informal **piles**) (British footballer [b. 1942])

north and south mouth

nose and chin **1** gin **2** a win (on a wager)

now and never clever

nuclear sub pub

Nuremberg trials haemorrhoids (informal **piles**) (trials of the principal leaders of Nazi Germany for war crimes at Nuremberg [1945-6])

O

ocean pearl girl

ocean wave a shave

Oedipus Rex sex (character in Greek mythology who, unaware of their relationship to him, kills his father and marries his mother)

oily rag cigarette (slang **fag**)

old fogey snot (vulgar slang **bogey**)

Old King Cole dole (unemployment benefit)

old nag cigarette (slang **fag**)

old pot and pan husband (**man**)

Oliver Twist drunk (vulgar slang **pissed**) (hero of the novel [1839] of the same name by Charles Dickens [1812-70])

on and off a cough

one another 1 mother 2 brother

open the door four

orchestra stalls testicles (vulgar slang **balls**)

Orinoco 1 cocoa 2 a poker (a river in Venezuela and Colombia)

Orphan Annie vagina (vulgar slang **fanny**)

over the stile committed for trial

Oxford bag cigarette (slang **fag**) (Oxford bags, trousers with very loose baggy legs, first popular in the 1920s)

Oxo cube the London Underground (informal **Tube**) (trade name of a kind of condensed stock sold in cubes for use in cooking)

PQR

After a heavy night of drinking never fear, I couldn't Adam and Eve it when I woke up the next day to find I'd left my rhythm and blues at the battle cruiser.

P

pain in the neck cheque

paper bag to nag

paper hat fool (slang **prat**)

paraffin lamp a tramp

Pat and Mick sick

Pat Cash act of urinating (vulgar slang **slash**) (Australian champion tennis player [b. 1965]))

peace and quiet a diet

pearly gate plate

Peckham Rye tie (neckwear) (district in Greater London)

pen and ink a stink

penny black the back

penny locket pocket

Peter Pan 1 a tan 2 a van (chief character in the play [1904] of the same name by J. M. [Sir James] Barrie [1860-1937])

Petticoat Lane pain (street and street market in East London)

philharmonic gin and tonic

Piccadilly silly
pick and choose alcohol, an alcoholic drink (slang **booze**)
pick up sticks six
pie and liquor vicar
pie and mash 1 cash 2 act of urinating (vulgar slang **slash**) 3 showy (slang **flash**)
pig's ear beer
pig's trotter a squatter
pillar and post ghost
pink lint penniless (slang **skint**)
plate and dish a wish
plates, plates of meat feet
Plymouth Argyll file (tool) (English football team)
poor relation station (railway)
pork chop police officer (slang **cop**)
port and brandy randy
pot and pan man, husband
pot of glue 1 clue 2 queue
pot of honey money
potted head dead

pound note a coat
pound of lead head
pounds and pence sense
pudding chef deaf
puddings and pies eyes
puff and drag a cigarette (slang **fag**)
Punch and Judy moody

Q
Queen's Park Rangers strangers
  (English football team)

R
rabbit hutch groin (**crotch**)
rain and pour to snore
Ramsgate Sands hands (the seaside
  resort, Ramsgate, Kent)
Raquel Welch a belch (US film star
  [b. 1940])
raspberry ripple nipple

raspberry tart a fart

rat and mouse a house

rattle and clank bank (financial)

rattle and jar car

read and write 1 to fight 2 escape (flight)

reeling and rocking stocking

rhythm and blues shoes

ribbon and curl girl (child)

rifle range change (money)

rip and tear to swear

rising damp cramp

River Ouse alcohol, an alcoholic drink (slang **booze**) (name of several English rivers)

River Tyne wine (a river in north-east England)

roast beef teeth

roast pork a fork

Robin Hood good

rock'n'roll dole (unemployment benefit)

rock of ages wages

rocks and boulders shoulders
roller coaster toaster
rolling billow a pillow
Ronnie Biggs lodgings (informal **digs**)
  (English criminal, one of the Great Train
  Robbers of 1963, recently returned to
  Britain to finish his prison sentence
  [b. 1929])
roof rack back
Rory O'Moore 1 floor 2 door 3 prostitute
  (**whore**)
rosie, Rosie Lee tea
Rosie O'Grady's women's toilet (**ladies'**)
round and square everywhere
round the houses trousers
Royal Mail bail
Royal Navy gravy
rub-a-dub a pub
rubber duck sexual intercourse (vulgar
  slang **fuck**)
Ruby Murray a curry (British popular
  singer [1935-96])

ruby red head
runner and rider cider
rusty nail gaol

STU

I had stopped for a top hat with my skin
and blister when her cheeky saucepan lid
brandy snapped me on the kingdom come
for half-inching his loop the loop.

S

sad and sorry lorry

safe and sound the ground

saint and sinner dinner

salmon and trout 1 tobacco (slang **snout**)
2 nose (informal **snout**) 3 stout (beer)
4 tout 5 gout

Santa's grotto drunk (slang **blotto**)

satin and silk milk

saucepan lid a child (informal **kid**)

sausage and mash 1 cash 2 car crash

sausage roll the dole (unemployment
benefit)

scarper, Scapa Flow to run away, get
out (**go**) (British naval anchorage in the
Orkney Islands, used in both world wars)

Scotch eggs legs

Sebastian Coe toe (British athlete and
politician [b. 1956])

seek and search church

Sexton Blake a fake (fictional detective
created by 'Hal Meredith' [Harry Blyth;

65

1852-98] in 1893
Sharon Stone a telephone (**phone**)
(US film star [b. 1957])
shepherd's pie the sky
Sherman tank an American (slang **Yank**)
(main battle tank of the Allies during the
Second World War; US-built)
shillings and pence sense
shiny and bright all right
shout and holler a collar
shovel and pick prison (slang **nick**)
shovels and spades AIDS
silver and gold old
skein of thread 1 bed 2 loaf of bread
skin and blister sister
sky rocket pocket
slip in the gutter butter
slug and snail fingernail
smack in the eye a pie
smash and grab taxi (**cab**)
smear and smudge a judge
snake in the grass 1 mirror (**looking**

glass) 2 drinking glass
snow and ice a price
soap and lather father
soap and water daughter
soapy bubble trouble
Sodom and Gomorrah to borrow (the biblical Cities of the Plain, destroyed by God for their wickedness [Genesis 19])
Southend Pier ear (at the English seaside resort of Southend-on-Sea, Essex)
Spanish Main a drain
spark and smoulder shoulder
spare rib a lie (informal **fib**)
spotted dick sick
stammer and stutter butter
stand at ease 1 cheese 2 fleas
Starsky and Hutch groin (**crotch**) (freelance detectives in the 1970s US TV series of that name)
Steffi Graf a laugh (German champion tennis player [b. 1969])

Steve McQueens jeans (Terence Steven McQueen, US film star [1930-80])
Stewart Granger danger (British-born [as James Stewart] film actor [1913-93])
stick of rock penis (vulgar slang **cock**)
sticks and stones bones
stocks and shares stairs
Stoke-on-Trent homosexual (slang **bent**)
stop and go toe
stop and start heart
storm and strife wife
strange'n'weird beard
struggle and strain 1 a train 2 to train
struggle and strife wife
sugar and honey money
sugar and spice 1 nice 2 ice
sunny south mouth
Suzie Wong a smell (slang **pong**) (from the film *The World of Suzie Wong* [1960], based on the novel by Richard Mason)
swallow and sigh collar and tie
swear and cuss (curse) bus

Sylvester Stallone alone (US film
  star [b. 1946])
syrup, syrup of figs wig

T
taxi rank bank (financial)
tea leaf thief
tent peg leg
Terry Waite late [British religious adviser
  held hostage in the Lebanon while
  negotiating the release of other hostages [b.
  1939])
there first a thirst
these and those clothes
thick and thin 1 a chin 2 gin 3 a grin
this and that 1 cat 2 hat 3 bat (cricket)
throw me in the dirt shirt
tickle your fancy male homosexual
  (slang **nancy**)
Tilbury Docks 1 socks 2 venereal
  disease (informal **pox**)

tin flute a suit

tin of beans jeans

tin tack dismissal from a job (informal **the sack**)

tin tacks facts

titfer, tit for tat hat

tit willow a pillow

to and fro snow

tod, Tod Sloane, on one's alone, on one's own

toilet roll dole (unemployment benefit)

tom, tomfoolery jewellery

Tom and Dick sick

tomato purée jury

Tom Mix 1 fix, predicament 2 six (US film actor, star of over 400 Westerns [1880-1940])

tommy guns diarrhoea (informal **the runs**) (from the Thompson submachine-gun, used by US gangsters and by the Allies during the Second World War)

Tommy Steele eel (stage name of Thomas

Hicks, British pop singer and actor
[b. 1936])

Tom Sawyer lawyer (hero of the novel
[1876] of the same name by the US writer
Mark Twain [Samuel Langhorne Clemens;
1835-1910])

Tony Benn ten pounds sterling (British
Labour politician [b. 1925])

Tony Blair hair (British Labour politician [b.
1953]; Prime Minister [1997-])

top hat 1 a chat 2 rat 3 fool (informal
prat)

Tower Bridge refrigerator (informal **fridge**)
(famous landmark and tourist attraction
spanning the Thames in London)

town crier liar

Trafalgar Square chair (Central London
landmark named after the British naval
victory over the French at Trafalgar [1805])

trolley and tram ham

trouble and strife 1 wife 2 life

troubles and cares stairs

Turkish bath a laugh
twist and twirl girl
two and eight nervous state
two-bob bit bowel movement (vulgar slang **shit**)
two-by-four prostitute (**whore**)
two eyes of blue! too true!
two-thirty dirty

U

ugly sister a blister
umbrella man, boyfriend (informal **fella**)
Uncle Bert shirt
Uncle Billy chilly
Uncle Ned 1 head 2 bed
Uncle Reg vegetables (informal **veg**)
up and under thunder
up a tree three

VW

She fell off her Vanity Fair and stormed off
in a cream puff when we all laughed. She
just couldn't see the egg yolk.

V

Vanity Fair chair (title of a novel [1848] by the English novelist William Makepeace Thackeray [1811-63]; the phrase comes from the allegory *A Pilgrim's Progress* [1678] by the English writer and preacher John Bunyan [1628-88])

Vera Lynn 1 gin 2 skin (Dame Vera Lynn, stage name of the British singer Vera Lewis [b. 1917], known as 'the Forces' Sweetheart' during the Second World War)

Vincent Price ice (US film star [1911-93])

W

Wallace and Gromit vomit (animated plasticine film characters created in the 1980s)

watch and chain brain

water hen ten

weasel and stoat coat

weeping willow pillow

Westminster Abbey taxi driver (informal **cabbie**) (famous Gothic church and tourist attraction in London)

whistle, whistle and flute a suit

White Cliffs of Dover over, finished

wick, Hampton Wick penis (vulgar slang **prick**) (village in Greater London)

wicked rumours women's knickers (informal **bloomers**)

Widow Twankey **1** handkerchief (informal **hanky**) **2** an American (slang **Yankee**) (comic character from the pantomime *Aladdin*)

William Tell a smell (early fourteenth-century semi-legendary Swiss patriot who reputedly shot an apple from his son's head with his crossbow)

wind and kite website

wooden plank an American (slang **Yank**)

woolly vest nuisance (**pest**)

working classes spectacles **(glasses)**
worry and strife wife
Wyatt Earp a belch (informal **burp**)
  (US lawman and gunfighter [1848-1929])

XYZ

I was just on my way out to didn't oughter the yours and ours in the beg your pardon, when, blow me if there wasn't a sudden bag of flour.

Yarmouth bloater car (informal **motor**)
yellow silk milk
Yorkshire tyke microphone (informal
  mike) (slang for someone from Yorkshire)
yours and ours flowers
Zane Grey wages (**pay**) (US writer of
  Westerns [1875-1939])

ENGLISH – RHYMING SLANG
ABC

Getting up the old apples when you've had a few Britney Spears and are feeling completely cream crackered is no bubble bath, believe you me.

A

advice lump of ice

AIDS shovels and spades

alcoholic (lush) comb and brush

all right harbour light; Isle of Wight; shiny and bright

alone Darby and Joan; Jack Jones, on one's; Sylvester Stallone; tod, Tod Sloane, on one's

American, Yank, Yankee board and plank; ham shank; Sherman tank; Widow Twankey; wooden plank

anus, arsehole, shitter Elephant and Castle; Gary Glitter

arm burglar alarm; false alarm; lucky charm

army daft and barmy; Kate Carney

aunt garden plant

B

back Cilla Black; haystack; penny black; roof rack

bad jack the lad

bad breath King Death
bail Royal Mail
baked beans kings and queens
balls, bollocks, knackers (testicles)
cheese and crackers; cobblers, cobbler's
awls; fun and frolics; Jackson Pollocks;
Max Walls; Niagara Falls; orchestra
stalls
bank (financial) Arthur Rank; cab rank;
iron tank; rattle and clank; taxi rank
bar bazaar; jack tar
barrow bow and arrow
basin Charley Mason; Fortnum & Mason
basinful (a great deal) Charley Mason
bat (cricket) this and that
bath hat and scarf
beard strange 'n' weird
bed born and bred; skein of thread;
Uncle Ned
beer Crimea; pig's ear
beer, pint of never fear
beers Britney Spears

belch Raquel Welch

believe Adam and Eve; Christmas Eve

bell hair gel

belly, stomach Auntie Nellie; Darby Kelly

bent, corrupt Clark Kent

berk, stupid person Berkeley Hunt;
Charlie Smirke

bet, flutter give and get; grumble and
mutter; house to let

bigot Lester Piggott

bike, bicycle clever Mike; do as you like;
Iron Mike

bird (woman) lemon curd

bitter (beer), pint of Gary Glitter; giggle
and titter; laugh and titter

blind bacon rind

blister brother and sister; ugly sister

boat frog in the throat; nanny goat

body hot toddy

bogey, snot old fogey

boil (spot) can of oil; Conan Doyle

bones sticks and stones

bonkers, crazy marbles and conkers
book Captain Cook
bookie, bookmaker cream cookie
boots daisy roots; King Canutes
borrow Sodom and Gomorrah
bottle Aristotle
bowel movement, dump Donald Trump
Boy Scout Brussels sprout
braces airs and graces; Epsom races
brain down the drain; watch and chain
brake (vehicle) Charlie Drake
brandy Charley Randy; fine and dandy;
   Mahatma Gandhi
bread needle and thread
break (free time) Charlie Drake
breast, titty Bristol, Bristol City; Mae
   West
breath life and death
bribe, bung Jimmy Young
brick Dublin trick
brothel flea and louse
brother one another

burp Wyatt Earp

burst Geoff Hurst

bus don't make a fuss; swear and cuss (curse)

butter Calcutta, cough and stutter; mutter and stutter; slip in the gutter; stammer and stutter

buttocks, arse, bum bubble gum; chorus and verse; fife and drum; kingdom come

button Len Hutton

C

cabbie (taxi driver) Westminster Abbey

cadge coat and badge

café Colonel Gaddafi

car, motor haddock and bloater; jam jar; la-di-dah; rattle and jar; Yarmouth bloater

car crash sausage and mash

cash, readies bangers and mash; dot and dash; Nelson Eddies; pie and mash;

sausage and mash

cat this and that

chair here and there; Lionel Blair;
  Trafalgar Square; Vanity Fair

chalk (used in billiards) Duke of York;
  Lambeth Walk

chance Charles Dance

change (money) rifle range

charabanc (coach) bow and arrow

chat top hat

cheat daisy beat

cheek hide and seek

cheese bended knees; cough and sneeze;
  flying trapeze; John Cleese; stand at ease

cheque chicken's neck; goose's neck;
  Gregory Peck; nervous wreck; pain in the
  neck

chief prison officer corned beef

child, kid, nipper dustbin lid; fly-tipper;
  God forbid; saucepan lid

chill frock and frill

chilly Uncle Billy

chin Errol Flynn; thick and thin
chip(s) (potato) Jagger's lips; jockey's whip
chum, friend finger and thumb
church seek and search
cider runner and rider
cigar la-di-dah
cigarette, fag oily rag; old nag; Oxford bag; puff and drag
cigarette lighter kung-fu fighter
cinema, pictures dolly mixtures
clever now and never
clothes these and those
clue, idea Danny La Rue; pot of glue
coal merry old soul
coat billy goat; nanny goat; pound note; weasel and stoat
cocaine, coke big bloke
cocoa Orinoco
cold brave and bold; Cheltenham gold
collar shout and holler
collar and tie swallow and sigh
comb garden gnome; ideal home

committed for trial over the stile
concertina constant screamer
cough Darren Gough; on and off
cousin baker's dozen
coward Charley Howard
cramp rising damp
crook babbling brook
cupboard Mother Hubbard
curry Ruby Murray

DEF

Some corned beef half-inched all my
Easter bunny, so I'm in soap and bubble
with the old fork and knife.

D

daft fore and aft

dance kick and prance

danger Stewart Granger

daughter bottle of porter; bottle of water; bricks and mortar; soap and water

dead brown bread; buttered bread; currant bread; gone to bed; potted head

deaf Mutt and Jeff; pudding chef

degree (university), first-class Geoff Hurst

degree (university), lower-second (2:2) Desmond

degree (university), third-class Douglas Hurd

detective, dick club and stick

diarrhoea, runs tommy guns

diet peace and quiet

dinner Charley Skinner; Jimmy Skinner; Michael Winner; saint and sinner

dirty two-thirty

disappear Brighton Pier

dish Lillian Gish

doddle (something simple) Glenn Hoddle

dog London fog

dole (unemployment benefit) cob o'coal; jam roll; Nat King Cole; Old King Cole; rock'n'roll; sausage roll; toilet roll

door Rory O'Moore

door-to-door salesman forty-four

dope (cannabis) bar of soap; Bob Hope

dough (money) cod's roe

drain Spanish Main

dress more or less

drill Benny Hill

drink, booze kitchen sink; pick and choose; River Ouse

dripping (fat) Doctor Crippen

drum finger and thumb

drunk, blotto, pissed, plastered booed and hissed; Brahms and Liszt; elephant's trunk; hand and fist; lord and mastered; Oliver Twist; Santa's grotto

E

ear bottle of beer; glass of beer; King Lear; Southend Pier

earner (profit-making scheme) Bunsen burner

easy ham and cheesy

eel Tommy Steele

egg borrow and beg

eight garden gate; Harry Tate

e-mail British Rail

employer, master lath and plaster

erection general election

everywhere round and square

excrement/excrete, shit, turd Douglas Hurd; Eartha Kitt; lemon curd; two-bob bit

exhausted, knackered Christmas crackered; cream crackered

eyes minces, mince pies; puddings and pies

F

face(s) airs and graces; Chevy Chase; deuce and ace; Epsom races; kipper and plaice

facts brass tacks; tin tacks

fake Sexton Blake

fanny (vagina) Orphan Annie

fare (transport) grey mare

fart apple tart; broken heart; D'Oyly Carte; horse and cart; Lionel Bart; raspberry tart

father soap and lather

favour Cheesey Quaver

feet dog's, dog's meat; plates, plates of meat

fight left and right; read and write

file (tool) Plymouth Argyll

fine (penalty) bottle of wine; Calvin Klein

fingernail slug and snail

fingers bell-ringers

fire Jeremiah; Molly McGuire

fish Lillian Gish

five Jack's alive; Lady Godiva; man alive

five pounds, fiver deep-sea diver; Lady Godiva

fix (predicament) Tom Mix

flares (flared trousers) Lionel Blairs

flea(s) Jennie Lee; Nancy Lee; stand at ease

flight (escape) read and write

floor Rory O'Moore

flower(s) happy hour; yours and ours

flu inky blue

food in the mood; in the nude

fool, chump, dope Joe Soap; lump and bump

fork Duke of York; roast pork

four door-to-door; knock at the door; open the door

fox Charles James (Fox)

fridge Tower Bridge

fuck, ride, shag goose and duck; Joe McBride; lame duck; Melvyn Bragg; rubber duck

GHI

What a giraffe! – that herring and kipper's run off with some ice-cream freezer in the pie and liquor's jam jar.

G

gaol ginger ale; jug and pail; moan and wail; rusty nail

garden beg your pardon; Dolly Varden

ghost pillar and post

gin Brian O'Flynn; needle and pin; nose and chin; thick and thin; Vera Lynn

gin and tonic philharmonic

girl ivory pearl; ocean pearl; ribbon and curl; twist and twirl

give over! Chatham and Dover

glass (drinking) snake in the grass

glasses (spectacles) working classes

gold hot and cold

good Robin Hood

gout salmon and trout

gravy Royal Navy

Greek bubble and squeak

grin thick and thin

groin, crotch rabbit hutch, Starsky and Hutch

ground safe and sound

H

haemorrhoids, piles chalfonts, Chalfont St Giles; Farmer Giles; Nobby Stiles; Nuremberg trials

hair barnet, Barnet Fair; Tony Blair

half cow and calf

ham trolley and tram

hand(s) brass band; Ramsgate Sands

handkerchief, hanky Widow Twankey

hard bread and lard

hat, lid ball and bat; God forbid; hard and flat; lean and fat; this and that; titfer, tit for tat

head ball of lead; cherry red; crust of bread; loaf, loaf of bread; pound of lead; ruby red; Uncle Ned

head of the family daily bread

heart horse and cart; stop and start

hill Jack and Jill

hole merry old soul

home, place drum and bass; ham and bone

horse bottle of sauce; Charing Cross

horse races airs and graces
house cat and mouse; flea and louse; rat and mouse
huff (bad temper) cream puff
husband, man old pot and pan; pot and pan

I

ice sugar and spice; Vincent Price
influenza, flu inky blue

JKL

I was having a quick jockey's whip after a
few kitchen sinks when I fell out of my
Lionel Blair and banged my loaf on the
Betty Grable.

J

jam baby's pram
jeans Steve McQueens; tin of beans
jelly Mother Kelly
Jesus Christ (in oaths) cheese and rice
jewellery tom, tomfoolery
job knocker and knob
joke can of Coke; egg yoke
judge Barnaby Rudge; smear and smudge
jury tomato purée

K

key(s) dancing fleas; Jennie Lee;
  knobbly knee
kipper Jack the Ripper
kiss hit and miss
knee(s) biscuits and cheese; Cecil Gee;
  chips and peas; high seas
knife charming wife; drum and fife;
  husband and wife; man and wife

L

ladies' (toilet) Rosie O'Grady's
lark (bird, prank) Noah's ark
late Harry Tate; Terry Waite
laugh bubble bath; cow and calf; giraffe;
  Steffi Graf; Turkish bath
lawyer Tom Sawyer
lazy Gert and Daisy
lazy person, skiver backseat driver
leg(s) bacon and eggs; clothes pegs; Dutch
  pegs; Easter egg; Mystic Meg; Scotch eggs;
  tent peg
letter Henrietta
liar Dunlop tyre; town crier
lie, fib collar and tie; spare rib
life fork and knife; trouble and strife
light Isle of Wight
liver bow and quiver; broken quiver
loaf of bread skein of thread
lodger artful dodger; Jolly Roger
lodgings, digs Ronnie Biggs
look butcher's, butcher's hook; Captain Cook

lorry sad and sorry
love heavens above

MNO

I've got my minces on a nanny goat for my old pot and pan, but I'm boracic till I get my greengages at the end of next bubble and squeak.

M

magistrate garden gate
mail, post Holy Ghost; Jimmy Nail
man, boyfriend, fella umbrella
mare Lionel Blair
margarine, marge little and large
married cash and carried
marry dot and carry
masturbate, wank Arthur Rank; Jodrell Bank
masturbator, wanker merchant banker
match itch and scratch
mate, friend china, china plate; Dutch,
  Dutch plate; garden gate
mean, tight inside right; Isle of Wight
meeting Buster Keaton
meter (gas, electricity etc.) Little Peter
microphone, mike Yorkshire tyke
milk satin and silk; yellow silk
minute (time) cock linnet
mirror, looking glass snake in the grass
money bees and honey; bread and honey;
  Bugs Bunny; Easter bunny; pot of honey;

sugar and honey
moody Punch and Judy
mother one another
mouth east and south; north and south;
 sunny south
muddle kiss and cuddle
mum (keep quiet) finger and thumb
murder iron girder

N

nag, scold paper bag
nark, police informer car park; Hyde
 Park; Noah's ark
neck bushel and peck; Gregory Peck
nerve, courage bottle, bottle and glass
nervous state two and eight
nice chicken and rice; sugar and spice
nicker (pound sterling) cherrypicker
nine Calvin Klein
nipple raspberry ripple
no Brown Joe

nonsense, rubbish cobblers, cobbler's
  awls
nose, snout salmon and trout
nuisance, pest woolly vest

O
off (stale) Frank Bough
old silver and gold
one (number) buttered bun
onions corns and bunions
over, finished White Cliffs of Dover
own, to be on one's on one's Jack Jones

PQR

The pork chops say that there's been a
couple of shifty Queen's Park Rangers
hanging around outside the rattle and
clank, so they're keeping their pudding and
pies on them.

P

pain Michael Caine; Petticoat Lane

pants, bloomers, knickers Alan Whickers;
  Brenda Frickers; wicked rumours

park Noah's ark

parole jam roll

parrot Jasper Carrott

party gay and hearty; hale and hearty

peep, look Bo Peep

penis, cock, dick, pecker, prick Black &
  Decker; bob and dick; Mars and Venus;
  stick of rock; wick, hampton, Hampton
  Wick

penniless, broke, skint Bernie Flint;
  boracic, boracic lint; heart of oak; pink
  lint

penny Abergavenny

pepper high-stepper

person, geezer fridge freezer; ice-cream
  freezer

piano Joanna

pickles Harvey Nichols

pie Captain Bligh; smack in the eye

pill Damon Hill; Jack and Jill; Jimmy Hill

pillow rolling billow; tit willow; weeping willow

plate Harry Tate; pearly gate

play night and day

please hairy knees

pocket chain and locket; Davy Crockett; penny locket; sky rocket

poker Orinoco

police officer, cop, copper bottle and stopper; ginger pop; pork chop

ponce, pimp Charlie Ronce

pong, smell Hong Kong; Suzie Wong

pony (twenty-five pounds) macaroni

pork Duke of York

port (wine) didn't ought

post (at a racecourse) Holy Ghost

pox, venereal disease boots and socks; cardboard box; Tilbury Docks

pram jar of jam

prat, fool paper hat; top hat

price snow and ice
priest bag of yeast
prison, nick cow's lick; shovel and pick
prison cell flowery dell
prostitute, whore boat and oar; forty-four; Rory O'Moore; two-by-four
pub, boozer battle cruiser; nuclear sub; rub-a-dub
publican, mine host dripping toast
pudding basin Fortnum and Mason
punter Billy Bunter
purse doctor and nurse

Q
queer (homosexual), bent, fairy, gay, nancy bottle of scent; Brighton Pier; Duke of Kent; ginger beer; Howard's Way; Julian Clary; King Lear; Milky Way; Stoke-on-Trent; tickle your fancy
queer (strange) ginger beer
queue pot of glue

R

rain, shower bag of flour; David Gower;
  Eiffel Tower; France and Spain; happy
  hour

randy Mahatma Gandhi; port and brandy

rat top hat

razor House of Fraser

rent Burton-on-Trent; Duke of Kent

ride Charlie Pride

right (side) Isle of Wight

ring Highland fling

road frog and toad

rotten Dolly Cotton

rough Brian Clough

round (of drinks) hare and hound

row, quarrel bull and cow

rum finger and thumb; kingdom come

run away, go scarper, Scapa Flow

STU

I was having a right old top hat with the bloke in the strange 'n' weird when that lemon curd splashed pig's ear all over my working classes.

S

sack (dismissal) tin tack
sale Jimmy Nail
scar Mars Bar
sense pounds and pence; shillings and
  pence
seven God in heaven
sex Oedipus Rex
sexual intercourse, ride Joe McBride
shandy Mahatma Gandhi
shark Noah's ark
shave dig a grave; ocean wave
shirt throw me in the dirt; Uncle Bert
shoes rhythm and blues
shoulder(s) rocks and boulders; spark and
  smoulder
showy, flash pie and mash
sick bob and dick; Moby Dick; Pat and
  Mick; spotted dick; Tom and Dick
silly Piccadilly
sing Highland fling
sister skin and blister

six chopping sticks; pick up sticks; Tom Mix
sixty-six clickety-click
skin Vera Lynn
sky shepherd's pie
slap brandy snap
sleep, kip Bo Peep; jockey's whip
slipper(s) big dippers; Jack the Ripper
smell heaven and hell; William Tell
smoke (cigarettes etc.) cough and choke;
  Joe Roke; laugh and joke
snake Joe Blake
sneeze breed and cheese
snore lion's roar; rain and pour
snow to and fro
snuff (tobacco) blindman's buff
soap Band of Hope; frisk and frolic
socks Tilbury Docks
son bath bun; Chelsea bun; currant bun
soup loop the loop
sparrow bow and arrow
spoon blue moon; Lorna Doone
squatter pig's trotter

squeal, inform on someone conger eel
stain Michael Caine
stairs apples, apples and pears; stocks and shares; troubles and cares
stale Jimmy Nail
starving Hank Marvin; Lee Marvin
station (railway) poor relation
steak Joe Blake
steal, pinch half-inch
stench Judi Dench
stink pen and ink
stinking Abraham Lincoln
stocking reeling and rocking
story Jackanory
stout (beer) salmon and trout
strangers Queen's Park Rangers
string Highland fling
stripper (striptease artiste) herring and kipper
suit bag of fruit; fiddle and flute; tin flute; whistle, whistle and flute
suitcase crowded space

sun bath bun; Chelsea bun; currant bun; hit and run

sunglasses, shades jack of spades

swear (curse) lord mayor; rip and tear

T

table Betty Grable; Cain and Abel

talk ball of chalk; Duke of York

talker, informer Johnnie Walker

tan (colour) Peter Pan

taxi, cab flounder and dab; Joe Baxi; smash and grab

tea glory be; Gypsy Rose Lee; Jennie Lee; Nancy Lee; rosie, Rosie Lee

teeth Bexleyheath; Hampstead Heath; roast beef

telephone, phone Darby and Joan; dog and bone; eau de cologne; ham and bone; Mike Malone; Sharon Stone

television, telly custard and jelly; Mother Kelly

ten Big Ben; cock and hen, cockle and hen; water hen

ten pounds, tenner Ayrton Senna; Big Ben; cock and hen, cockle and hen; Tony Benn

theatre box Charles James (Fox)

thief corned beef; leg of beef; tea leaf

thin needle and pin

thirst Geoff Hurst; there first

thirty Burlington Bertie

three up a tree

throat nanny goat

thunder up and under

ticket bat and wicket

tie (neckwear) Peckham Rye

tights fly-by-nights

till (cash) Benny Hill; Jack and Jill

time (prison sentence) bird, birdlime; grease and grime

toast Holy Ghost

toaster roller coaster

tobacco, snout salmon and trout

toe(s) buttons and bows; Sebastian Coe; stop and go

toilet, bog captain's log

tomato sauce dead horse

tongue Jimmy Young

too true! two eyes of blue!

tools crown jewels

tote (betting system) canal boat; nanny goat

tout salmon and trout

town Joe Brown

traffic warden Gay Gordon

train John Wayne; struggle and strain

train, to struggle and strain

trainer (shoe) Claire Rayner

tram jar of jam

tramp hurricane lamp; paraffin lamp

transport, wheels jellied eels

trouble soapy bubble

trousers, pants fleas and ants; insects and ants; round the houses

trowel Baden-Powell

true Irish stew

truth Maud and Ruth
twelve, dozen country cousin; monkey's
   cousin
twenty horn of plenty
twins needles and pins
tyre Billy Liar

U

umbrella Auntie Ella
Underground (London), Tube Oxo cube
understand, twig earwig
**urine/urinate/urination, leak, pee,
   piddle, pish/piss, slash** bangers and
   mash; bubble and squeak; Christopher
   Lee; gypsy's kiss; hit and miss; Jimmy
   Riddle; Leslie Ash; Lillian Gish; Pat Cash;
   pie and mash

VW

This new whistle fits me like a second Vera Lynn – mind you, I paid a lot of Bugs Bunny for it.

V

van Peter Pan
vegetables, veg Uncle Reg
vest east and west
vicar pie and liquor
villain Harold Macmillan
vomit Wallace and Gromit

W

wad (roll of banknotes) Ken Dodd
wager John Major
wages, pay greengages; rock of ages; Zane
   Grey
waistcoat Charlie Prescott
waiter cheese grater; cold potato
walk ball of chalk; Duke of York
water didn't oughter; dirty daughter;
   fisherman's daughter; miller's daughter
website wind and kite
week bubble and squeak
whiskers hammer and discus

whisky, Scotch Charley Frisky; gay and
   frisky; gold watch
wife, missus bread knife; carving knife;
   drum and fife; Duchess of Fife; fork and
   knife; hugs and kisses; joy of my life; kiss
   of life; love and kisses; storm and strife;
   struggle and strife; trouble and strife;
   worry and strife
wig(s) guinea pig; Irish jig; syrup, syrup of
   figs
win nose and chin
wind (flatulence) Jenny Lind
window burnt cinder
wine Calvin Klein; River Tyne
winner hot dinner
wish plate and dish
word dicky-bird; early bird
wrong Hong Kong

XYZ

That poncy Yarmouth bloater of his cost
him more than a year's Zane Grey, but
you wouldn't catch me taking a Charlie
Pride in it.

Y

yes Brown Bess
yuppie Hush Puppy

A graduate of Edinburgh University, **Betty Kirkpatrick** is a writer, editor, compiler, journalist and occasional broadcaster. Her major works include *The Oxford Paperback Thesaurus*, *Chambers Twentieth-Century Dictionary*, *Roget's Thesaurus*, *Cassell's Concise Dictionary*, and Bloomsbury's *Dictionary of Clichés*, and she has been a contributor to many other leading dictionaries and reference works. Since 1981, she has made occasional broadcasts on language-related topics for the BBC, and has been the words columnist of the Glasgow *Herald* newspaper from 1981-94 and 1997 to date. She is also the author of *The Little Book of Scottish Grannies' Remedies*, *The Little Book of Irish Grannies' Remedies*, *The Little Book of Scottish Wit and Wisdom*, and *The Little Book of Irish Wit and Wisdom*, all published by Michael O'Mara Books Ltd.

The Little Book of Totally Stupid Men – ISBN 1-85479-833-2
The Little Book of Despair – ISBN 1-85479-818-9
The Little Book of Tantric Sex for Busy People –
   ISBN 1-85479-685-2
The Little Book of Sex Fantasies – ISBN 1-85479-725-5

The Little Book of Minge Topiary – ISBN 1-84317-051-5 (£2.99)

New, expanded 128-page editions.
All at £2.50 each including postage (UK only).

The Little Book of Farting – ISBN 1-85479-445-0
The Little Book of Stupid Men – ISBN 1-85479-454-X
The Little Toilet Book – ISBN 1-85479-456-6
The Little Book of Cockney Rhyming Slang – 1-84317-027-2
The Little Book of Crap Excuses – ISBN 1-84317-040-X
The Little Book of Crap Advice – ISBN 1-84317-041-8
LUVTLK! ltle bk of luv txt – ISBN 1-84317-042-6
Dirty Cockney Rhyming Slang – ISBN 1-84317-035-3
The Little Book of Speed Dating – ISBN 1-84317-074-4
The Little Book of Dirty Speed Dating – ISBN 1-84317-080-9
WAN2TLK? ltle bk of txt msgs – ISBN 1-84317-082-5

All Michael O'Mara titles are available by post from:

Bookpost, PO Box 29, Douglas, Isle of Man IM99 1BQ

Credit cards accepted.

Telephone: 01624-677237
Fax: 01624-670923
E-mail: bookshop@enterprise.net
Internet: www.bookpost.co.uk
Free postage and packing in the UK.